Nathaniel Brassey Halhed, Governor Johnstone

A Letter to Governor Johnstone

On Indian Affairs

.

Nathaniel Brassey Halhed, Governor Johnstone

A Letter to Governor Johnstone
On Indian Affairs

ISBN/EAN: 9783744764032

Printed in Europe, USA, Canada, Australia, Japan

Cover: Foto ©ninafisch / pixelio.de

More available books at **www.hansebooks.com**

A

LETTER

T O

Governor Johnſtone, &c. &c.

O N

INDIAN AFFAIRS.

Ne quid detrimenti Reſpublica caperet.

PRINTED FOR S. BLADON, IN PATER-NOSTER-ROW.
MDCCLXXXIII.

A

LETTER

T O

GOVERNOR JOHNSTONE,

&c. &c.

S I R,

BY the prevalence of popular prejudice,
and the contention of rival interests, by
the unqualified affertions of a few defigning
individuals, and the defective ftate of general
information, has the Eaft-India Company been
reduced to almoft inextricable difficulties.
In the hour of difmay, and in her laft ftruggle
for expiring rights, had not You voluntarily
and vigoroufly ftepped forth to her affiftance,
fhe would, ere the prefent moment, have

become the fervile tool of arbitrary power, or the paffive victim of hungry Faction.— Alternately threatened and cajoled, fleeced and reviled, fcrutinized and mifunderftood, too long has fhe filently wept over the infringements of her privileges, the mutilation of her charters, the difturbance of her arrangements, and the difpofal of her property. Every fyftem of policy, every plan of commerce, every principle of action, by which (in conformity to frequent acts of the legiflature, and under, the immediate encouragement of charters from the Crown) the profperity of our affairs in Afia has gradually augmented the trade, the power, and the refources of the Mother Country, fo as to become one of the moft important pledges for the ftability of the empire, have been violently and repeatedly explored, to gratify a malignant, or an interefted curiofity. Every record which might difplay the fources from whence are derived the Company's wealth and dominion, has been wantonly torn from its facred repofitory, and circulated in reports and appendixes through the whole European world. By thefe means have her councils been diftracted at home, and her defigns

fruftrated

fruftrated abroad : The chain of mutual de-
pendance, which bound up all her fervants
into one connected body, and directed the
aggregate impulfe of their united exertions to
the one grand object of the Company's fuccefs, has been broken : Her vigilant and in-
veterate enemies, by thus acquiring a knowledge of her intentions, of her preparations,
and of her poffible refources, have been inftructed to evade, to counteract, to overturn
all her fchemes, and to purfue their own in
full fecurity ; while her immediate agents by
fuggeftions, by menaces, by temptations, have
been feduced into a partial departure from the
ftrait outline of their delegated functions ;
have been encouraged in meafures hoftile to
their beft fervants abroad, and deftructive
of all their own official confequence. In this
perilous fituation, while war preys on her
extremities, and influence corrodes her vitals,
languifhing equally under the feverity of her
diforder, and the infidious prefcriptions of
her political empiricks, has your animated
affiftance exhilarated her with a new and un-
expected chance for life. The tafk you have
undertaken is not lefs toilfome than generous ;
frefh impediments will inceffantly retard your

progrefs

[4]

progrefs—difficulty will ftart out of difficulty, and labour beget labour. After all, the fubject is fo complex, the drama is fo wound up with danger and diftrefs, that imagination itfelf can fcarcely invent for it (within the limits of human probability) a fafe and a . fatisfactory cataftrophe to either of the parties. What *can* be done, You will do—and I doubt not, but the ftrength and fteadinefs of your efforts will as much do credit to your head, as the voluntary liberality of your interpofition has already diftinguifhed your heart. If I have taken the liberty to prefent you here with a few reflections, they are not fuch as I can for a moment fuppofe may conduce to your better information, but they may ultimately advance my own and that of the public; for wherever I fhall have been wrong, I truft implicitly to your future orations, in the courfe of the enfuing debates, for correction; and I flatter myfelf, that upon the whole, I fhall have contributed fome fmall portion to that general mafs of knowledge which muft, or which ought to be collected, before the final decifion of one of the moft important topics that ever was agitated in the council of the nation.

To

To me the fyftematic regularity neceffary
for the well-doing of a body conftituted like
the Eaft-India Company, where commerce
and politicks are fo intimately interwoven,
feems to be as much liable to danger from
too frequent inftances of parliamentary inter-
ruption, as her independent rights from the
encroaching patronage of the Crown. No
doubt we more immediately feel an arbitrary
fummons, which difplaces our firft confidential
fervants, and obtrudes on us others, in whom
(however worthy) we cannot at once repofe
that implicit confidence which long-tried fide-
lity alone can juftify : But to have our fecrets
expofed, our plans fufpended, our Directors
intimidated, and our arrangements thrown
into confufion by reiterated formalities of
legiflative inveftigation, tends ultimately to
damp the fpirit of mercantile enterprife, to
difcompofe that orderly mechanifm which is
the very foul of an extenfive trade, and to
clog all the intricate operations of credit.
You, Sir, have undoubtedly traced the Company in her filent progrefs towards maturity,
and to that fplendor which rendered her an
object for minifterial concupifcence. You
have

have obferved how an unforefeen ftroke of misfortune laid her in a fupplicating pofture at the feet of Adminiftration, in 1772; and I think you will agree with me that fhe then paffed her grand climaƌerick, never again to recover her youthful health or vigour. To that unfortunate inftant, when a temporary convention was fubftituted in the place of a conclufive treaty, when her embarraffed affairs were thrown on the Speaker's table as a perpetual tub for the patriotic whale, moderate and thinking men will afcribe the too evident fymptoms of her probable diffolution; and why? Becaufe Parliament has too often chofen to put itfelf in the place of the Company, without having the leifure neceffary for an adequate attention to its affairs; becaufe too frequent revifion breaks the thread of progreffive aƌion; and becaufe, when old fyftems are overturned, eftablifhed regulations fuperfeded, and new experiments obtruded upon ancient habits, reform is but another name for diforder; becaufe an aƌ of Parliament, empowering the Crown to grant the Company a renewal of their charter for ten years, feems a kind of national warrant for the uninterrupted exercife of all the func-

tions,

tions, and enjoyment of all the privileges conferred by that charter for those ten years; becaufe, in fhort, the very principle, that Parliament has a right at every turn of affairs to interfere in the internal managements of the Eaft-India Company (however true and juft as far as refpects parliamentary omnipotence) may perhaps be deemed extremely inexpedient in its effects, and liable to be converted into a moft dangerous inftrument for the purpofes of faction, of avarice, or of ambition. The continuation or removal of the Governor-general of Bengal is but the tool of the prefent hour, and of the prefent workmen. The mine will ftill be rich, when the ore now working fhall be exhaufted: other adventurers will prefently difcover a frefh vein. It is the *principle* that I wifh to combat: it is not a victory in favour of this or that rival for government, that can effectually ferve the Company, but a decided acknowledgement of her rights as held under Royal Charter, of her independence for a certain number of years as fanctioned and fecured by act of Parliament. But as the name of Haftings has already furnifhed the word for attack, it muft

now

now become alfo the fignal for defence. If
a corporate body, like the Eaft-India Company, be liable to thefe inceffant fhocks,
where is the liberty of the fubject, where
the faith of the Crown, where the ftability
of law ? *The next blow may be on the Bank.*
We can all recollect the wonderful revolution
that took place in the Company's property,
by the act of 13. Geo. III. when the qualification which fhould entitle a proprietor to
vote, was raifed from five hundred pounds to
one thoufand pounds ftock, and when the
duration of the office of Director was pro-
longed from one year to four. Before that
memorable æra, a qualification to vote was
as much my property as a freehold ; and the
regular change of Directors, by a fyftem of
annual rotation, was thought the palladium
which would ever preferve the proprietary
from a grafping ariftocracy. We may perhaps, foon hear of quadrennial or perpetual
Bank Directors—we may have a Governor of
the Bank by Act of Parliament, and only
removeable with the approbation of the
Crown. It is vain to urge the difference of
the cafe, with refpect to the two Companies,
while they both hold their exiftence on the

fame

fame tenure, a Royal Charter. The law, which difcriminates not between rich and poor, is equally indifferent to all other accidents of circumftance, where the bafis of the claim is one and the fame. Each of thefe grand members of the State owes its original eftablifhment to the voluntary combination of private merchants. The India Company's powers were as explicit as thofe of the Bank, and the purpofes of its inftitution as well defined. They were to fit out fhips for an Eaftern commerce, and fhift for themfelves in an unknown world. Events gave them power and wealth, and their acquifitions are fo much clear gain to the State. But now that they have raifed a fortune, they muft confent to have it managed by *ftrange* ftewards. What bulwark has the Bank againft fimilar treatment? *That* body too, has rifen to a pitch of wealth and confeqnence unfufpeated by its firft contrivers: why fhould no patriot find it convenient to call for a revifion of its ftatutes, an examination of its accounts, and a ftatement of its annual profits? No doubt he might difcover, that it could well afford a falary of five or ten thoufand pounds per annum to its Governor;

nor

nor would he want a plea to propofe himfelf,
or his coufin, or his informer, to the office,
and to conftitute it an eftablifhment for life.
One ftretch of prerogative authorizes another.
If the Eaft India Company muft be fettered
in the *appointment* of their Governor-General
of Bengal, or of any their fervants, civil or
military, they cannot long expect to hold the
power of *difmiffion*; which if it be once
wrefted from them, their influence and authority in the directing, ordering, and management of their affairs, commercial as well as
political, will be utterly annihilated. Yet
why fhould Miniftry content themfelves with
the fingle act of oppofing the Company's
wifhes for the continuation of their Governor-
General? It would be a curious fpeculation
to reverfe the inftance, and fuppofe, that the
Court of Proprietors having come to a pe-
remptory refolution of recalling a Governor,
Miniftry had forbidden the difpatch of the
neceffary paragraphs——how inftantaneous
would be the Company's ruin on fuch an
event, I need not attempt to delineate; and
yet we are at this moment treading on the
very brink of the precipice! But grant that
the Crown means in future to be more reten-
tive

tive of its interference, and ſhall hereafter
adhere cloſely to the letter and ſpirit of that
claufe in the Regulating Act of Parliament,
which limits its powers of prohibition *to
articles immediately relating to war and peace.*—
Still, if it ſhall be in the habit of taking um-
brage at every act of the Company, which it
ſhall chufe to confider as refractory, or un-
accommodating, and in apparent warmth of
temper, determine to make all ſuch queſtions
the objects of parliamentary difcuſſion, the
ſpirit of conſtitutional reſiſtance, and virtuous
inflexibility, will at length be worn out in the
conteſt, or the confuſion of perpetual and
harraſſing references throw the Company's
affairs into a ſtate of bankruptcy.

The Court of Proprietors is the delibe-
rative body, the parliament of the Company;
the Directors are its miniſtry. In them is
lodged the executive power, and it is necef-
ſary that they ſhould not be too often
changed, left the courfe of public bufineſs
be thereby impeded. The patriots of the
preſent hour call loudly for an annual repre-
ſentation in Parliament, on the idea that every
man of common fenfe is qualified to give his

opinion

opinion without ferving an apprenticefhip. On the fame principle the Company's affairs would not be interrupted, if each quarterly General Court produced a new fet of Proprietors. But neither Parliament nor Proprietors could with fafety venture to affume to themfelves the management of the detail, and the functions of their Minifters and Directors. It is only in the grand outlines of conduct, in the leading features of the fyftem, that the collective body can or ought to exert its powers of controul; but *then* its language is abfolute, its commands irrefiftible, and obedience unconditional. " The inde-" pendence of America," fays the national voice, " is become a meafure neceffary for " the falvation of this country." " We " infift upon an explicit recognition of " American independence," echoes the Parliament—Minifters figh, and acquiefce ; and yet we all know the fentiments of the Crown. " Mr. Haftings is the only man," fay the Company, " who, in the prefent pofture of " our Afiatic affairs, is qualified to be Go-" vernor-General of Bengal." " We think it " advifable to remove him," reply the Directors.

rectors. " We pofitively forbid you," re-
join the Proprietors, *fix to one.* " It is againft
" the wifh of the two Chairs," anfwer the
Directors, " but we muft fubmit." Here
is no fophiftry, no trick, no management;
a plain queftion is agitated in a public and
peaceable affembly : reafon operates on their
underftandings, and their refolution is the
refult of calm conviction. " Mr. Haftings,"
fay the Directors, " has been cenfured by
" two refpectable Committees of the Houfe
" of Commons. On *their* reports the Houfe
" has judged him worthy of recall, and we
" therefore recall him." The Proprietors,
in anfwer, urge, " That Mr. Haftings has
" been accufed of opinions which he did
" not profefs, and of acts which he did not
" command; of wars, whofe commence-
" ment was equally out of his knowledge,
" and againft his advice ; of revolutions, to
" which he contributed nothing but perfonal
" rifk and a miraculous efcape; and of
" defpotifm, of difobedience, and fundry
" indefinite charges, whofe impenetrable ob-
" fcurity alone fecures them from flat con-
" tradiction. If the Houfe of Commons,
" in

" in voting his recall*, mean to influence
" our councils, or dictate to our Directors,
" it

* It is worthy of remark, that the vote for the recall
of Mr. Haftings, that loaded him with undefined
charges, was never debated at the Secret Committee;
a fact not generally known. It was indeed brought
forward under that impreffion, as a kind of compromife,
and may be fairly termed a parliamentary juggle. On
the 14th of May laft, in the Rockingham adminiftration, when Mr. Burke and Mr. Fox were in the plenitude of power, Sir Adam Ferguffon, the Lord Advocate
being abfent, (after a conference in the Houfe of Commons with Mr. Fox, Mr. Burke, and Gen Smith) propofed to a Committee of the whole Houfe, that the
forty-four refolutions which had been brought forward by
the Secret Committee fhould be voted. When the Houfe
had gone through them, Sir Adam propofed another,
in fubftance as follows; " That it was the duty of the
" Court of Directors to remove thofe perfons whom the
" Houfe of Commons had cenfured." Mr. Robinfon,
member for Canterbury, obferved upon this occafion,
that the Houfe *was rather thin*, confidering the importance of the refolution. It paffed, however, there
being at the time *twenty-eight* members in the Houfe.
This refolution, if carried into effect, would have re-
moved every man in power in India ; perhaps this might
be the reafon that it never was reported to the Houfe,
though a refolution of what is termed a Committee of
the whole Houfe. On the 28th of May the Lord
Advocate brought forward his refolution for the recall
of

" it hath exceeded its jurifdiction. We are
" Proprietors of the territories of Bengal,
" &c. for a certain number of years, under
" the moft facred of all compacts, the pledge
" of the Royal Charter, and the authority of
" the whole Legiflature. If our Governor
" be criminal, he is at all times amenable to
" the laws of his country. If there be
" grievances, we who are his immediate maf-
" ters are the perfons aggrieved : If there be
" wrongs, we have both the will and the
" means to redrefs them.—We have feen
" none.—You and your Committees have
" not as yet proved a tittle againft him :
" The *onus probandi* certainly lies on the ac-
" cufers.—Shew why we ought to remove
" him, and we will do it upon evidence : In
" the mean time, we deem it abfolutely ne-
" ceffary for our immediate exigencies that
" he fhould continue in the Chair."——In
this ftate of the bufinefs the Crown unex-
pectedly

ef Mr. Haftings and Mr. Hornby, and it was carried,
there being at the time *forty-two* members in the
Houfe. Mr. Fox fpoke upon the occafion, allowed
Mr. Haftings to poffefs both abilities and integrity, but
voted for his removal, becaufe his plan of politics had
been difapproved of.

pectedly interferes: Parties grow warm: Miniftry enter the lifts againft Mr. Haftings;
the Company, alarmed at the imminent danger of their moft important rights, feel their
very exiftence to depend on his fupport.
The matter is thrown into Parliament; a
thoufand difcordant interefts will be impli-
cated in the ftruggle, and You, Sir, nobly
undertake the caufe of abfent merit. It is
not the leaft wonderful part of the fpectacle,
to obferve Miniftry and Oppofition taking the
fame fide of the queftion for Mr. Haftings's
recall, on pleas totally contradictory. But
though the object be different, the paffion,
you will fay, is ftill the fame. Miniftry contend for *patronage*, the other party toil for
bread: and thus it is, that the eagernefs of
each prevents them from taking notice of
their inconfiftency; and that while both are
fighting their adverfary's battles in an unna-
tural confederacy, the very means by which
they feparately pufh the fame point, precifely
counteract each other's views. " The Mini-
" fter intends to caft a veil over Eaft-India
" delinquency," fays Oppofition, by way of
ftimulus to the attack. " *The abufes and dif-*
" *orders which prevail in the Bengal Govern.*
" *ment*

" ment, the various, heavy, and complicated op-
" preſſions which the natives ſuffer under them,
" deſpotiſm over the ſubjects abroad, diſobedience
" to the government of this country, and a waſte of
" public treaſure for private purpoſes, cry aloud for
" juſtice on the delinquent." " Mr. Haſtings,"
adds the foaming orator, " is that delinquent.
" I ſtake my character againſt his, and
" pledge myſelf to produce evidence of
" facts." " I renounce," replies the Mini-
ſterial Mouth-piece, " all idea of delinquency:
" I have borne teſtimony to the merit and
" the integrity of the Governor-General,
" but I would recall him on the principle of
" expediency: and I flatter myſelf that I ſhall
" demonſtrate this expediency to the ſatis-
" faction of the Houſe." Can thoſe who
hold out Mr. Haſtings as a culprit, and thoſe
who acquit him of all ſuſpicion of culpability,
unite in the ſame vote? Will thoſe independent ſenators, who ſhall remark ſuch palpable contradictions and glaring prejudices,
cordially join with either? Forbid it, reaſon
and common ſenſe! Forbid it, public juſtice and
national honour!—The die, however, is now
caſt, and the parties have gone too far to recede:
the different queſtions of expediency and of de-

linquency

linquency muft feverally be brought before
the Houfe, and I hope not before empty
benches* ; but who fhall guefs at the fen-
tence, when we know not even the exact
counts of the indictment?

It is generally conjectured that the *accufation* will confift of two members, and that
an elaborate, extravagant, tragi-comic ha-
rangue will firft expatiate upon " the extra-
" ordinary expulfion of a Rajah of the higheft
" rank, &c. &c. from his dominions;" and
next, *on a fecret article* permitted to be con-
ditionally inferted in an intended treaty with
the Rajah of Berar, of which he never received the flighteft hint. On the firft point
it will be argued (with a proper quantity of
pathetic interludes and theatrical apoftrophes)
that the Governor-General had no right to
propofe exacting a fine of fifty lacks of rupees from Rajah Cheyt Sing: that he had no
right to demand a fum for contingent ex-
pences of the war over and above his ftipu-
lated

* Twenty-eight members only were in the Houfe
when Sir Adam Ferguffon's forty-fifth refolution paffed,
and forty-two when the vote for the recall of Mr.
Haftings and Mr. Hornby was propofed and carried,

lated rent, and that he had no right on any grounds to expel him from his hereditary estate; perhaps alfo that he had no right to advance the rents upon his fucceffor. In the fecond article will probably be urged the fatal policy of uniting the formidable powers of the Mahrattas under one active command, the danger of drawing on ourfelves the vengeance of the Nizam, fhould we encourage Boofla to invade his dominions, and the confequences of that grand alliance of the Afiatic Princes formed under *his* aufpices as a counterbalance to Britifh influence. The above are, as far as I can judge, the *ftrong grounds* of the *criminatory party.* It has been remarked, Sir, upon the fubject of your late admirable oration in Leadenhall-ftreet, that Mr. Haftings's friends have felected all the ftrong points of argument which the fubject afforded, and *made the moft of them.* Now I apprehend, that You, and all thofe whom conviction has engaged in that gentleman's defence, would fcout the obfervation with contempt. They have not *felected* the ftrong points, but the cafe afforded no other. They have combated fophiftry by fimple proofs,

and

and wanton falfehoods by plain matter of
fact. His enemies have had all the choice
of fubject : they have taken up fuch points as,
to their jaundiced eye, appeared to afford the
moft colour; and to fay the truth, *They
have made the moft of them.* For they have
afferted delinquency where they have yet to
prove error : they undauntedly urge the
fame fophifticated tale after twenty refuta-
tions : and but the other day their *cloud-com-
pelling champion* exaggerated the *vifionary* objects of the Governor-General's oppreffion to
thirty millions. This is *making the moft* of a
point, with a vengeance! And yet he had
recently before his eyes his topographical
friend's excellent delineation, where he might
trace the progrefs of the Governor-General's
glory to the very fartheft limits of its influence, though the page ungeneroufly funk
his name; and where he might have learned
the ftate of population in Bengal fufficiently
to have kept himfelf within the bounds of
oratorical probability. But to our argument.

When

When the Governor-General fet out on his journey for Benares, Cheyt Sing's preparations for revolt were almoft at the point of maturity; of which no evidence can be more fully illuftrative, than the number of his troops, the condition of his forts, and the plenitude of his magazines, as difcovered in the courfe of the revolution. Mr. Haftings, in the true fpirit of candour, has informed the public of his intention to have affeffed the Raja in a fine of forty or fifty lacks of rupees, but Cheyt Sing never gave him time to propofe a fyllable of fuch his purpofe. While he meant to have lulled the Governor-General's vigilance for a few days with the fubmiffion of a well-acted repentance, the fuddennefs of his arreft precipitated all his fchemes, and probably faved the Governor's life. Had the Raja's guilty confcience permitted him to perfevere in his affected docility of conduct, had he quietly paid the fine, and fuffered the unfufpecting victim to depart from Benares without alarm, there can hardly be a doubt but fome of his numerous ambufcades of banditti might have maffacred the Governor-General and his whole efcort, before they could poffibly reach Chunar.

Chunar. But the providential arreft difcon-
certed all Cheyt Sing's cool-blooded hypo-
crify, and while it certainly anticipated the
hour of rebellion *, ferved perhaps as an additional

---

* A few individuals among us make no fcruple to
infinuate, that Cheyt Sing had no premeditated plan of
rebellion, and that his conduct was the refult of inftant
refentment and defpair on his arreft. But on thofe per-
verted minds, which a perufal of Mr. Haftings's candid
narrative of the tranfactions at Benares, together with
its appendix, fhall not have awakened to the palpable
impoffibility, that a body of armed men, fo numerous
and well appointed, as that which affifted in the Raja's
efcape, and perpetrated the maffacre of our troops,
fhould have been inftantly affembled on the fpur of the
occafion, without long-prepared and deep-laid defign,
neither argument nor proof will make any impreffion.

Thofe who can reprefent Cheyt Sing's rebellion as
the impulfe of the moment, may well deny the glaring
intrigues of the two plotting Begums of Oude, and the
dangerous fpirit of defection, which their machinations
had raifed in the Vizier's dominions.

To the author of fuch wretched furmifes, I leave it
to enjoy the contemptible triumph of diffembled dif-
belief. I have no pleafure in purfuing phantoms; a
refutation of his affertions is my prefent purpofe, not a
reformation of his underftanding or principles. In addition to the connected feries of deduction, by which
Cheyt Sing's motives are indifputably demonftrated
from

ditional ſtimulus to the revolt of his deluded
followers. You, Sir, have eſtabliſhed be-
yond

from his actions, and to the ſeveral reſpectable. teſti-
monials which have already appeared to confirm each
part of the charge, I ſhall here quote the following
document, which has not yet been made public,
but of which the authentic record may be peruſed at
the India-Houſe.

Extract of a letter from Mr. John Holland, our Re-
ſident at the Nizam's Court, to the Governor-general,
and Supreme Council of Bengal, dated Hydrabad,
8th October, 1781. Entered in Bengal Conſultations,
29th October, 1781.

After ſtating what the Nizam had ſaid to him the pre-
ceding day, relative to the hoſtile diſpoſition of the Mahrattas, which the Nizam had learned from the Mahratta
Miniſter, Mr. Holland adds theſe words, " His High-
" neſs ſaid, that the (Mahratta) Miniſter had inform-
" ed him of *a plan of general attack* upon our poſſeſ-
" ſions : one numerous army of horſe had been ap-
" pointed to the ſervice of laying waſte our Circars ;
" another with Booſla and other Mahratta Chiefs,
" was to enter Bongal by the way of Cuttack, and a
" third, Scindia's, &c. was to proceed from Malva,
" *to ſupport the inſurrection of Cheyt Sing, and other*
" *Zemindars,* to join Nujuff Cawn, and to penetrate
" into the heart of the Bengal Provinces."

Cheyt Sing was arreſted the 18th of Auguſt. This
letter is dated the 8th of October—an interval of only
forty-

yond the possibility of cavil, in your late forcible speech to the Court of Proprietors, that the

forty-nine days, in which it was barely possible, that the account of the arrest should travel from Benares to Hydrabad; but which utterly precludes the probability of the Nizam's having received from thence, letters of any later date, with information of those very extensive military preparations which the Raja was subsequently discovered to have secretly arranged—much less that he should have *then* have obtained accurate intelligence of those facts, which afterwards proved the existence of a very powerful disaffected party in Oude, fomented by the two ambitious Begums, to which Mr. Holland's letter most indubitably alludes.

The conversation here related, passed on the 7th of October, and was in consequence of a *previous* conference between the Nizam and the Mahratta Minister, to whom also we must allow some time for receiving and connecting his intelligence from different quarters; which will carry back the dates so far, as to leave a clear impossibility for any part of this account to have been the produce of *ex post facto* information.

But when we consider, that the Mahratta Minister's communication to the Nizam, was not of detached scraps of intelligence, derived to himself from various channels, but of a deliberate connected plan of conduct, severally agreed to by different powers, at almost the different extremities of India; and that this circumstantial account could only have come to the Minister from

his

the Governor-General, as reprefentative of Cheyt Sing's immediate paramount, had a clear right to infift on his provifional aid for the general burthen of the war. It is a right, Sir, coeval with the exiftence of all Government; and as it is authorized by plain reafon, and the very nature of things, fo it is warranted by precedents from the Mogul hiftory. Under the proof of this right is comprehended a full conviction of the Raja's culpability in refiftance. To fuch culpability, and for fuch a culprit, what is the adequate, the convenient, and, I may add, the only conftitutional mode of punifhment?—A fine : and what the *ultima ratio* of feodal authority ?—Difpoffeffion. You will here naturally recollect a paragraph which I have quoted in my fixth letter, in the Morning Herald—It is as follows :

E

Extract

his principles at Poona, we muft of neceffity allow a date of fome months at leaft, to the Machiavelian bafis of Cheyt Sing's infurrection, founded on the known diffaffection of the two Begums, and on expectations of great collateral affiftance, in confequence of a general compact for our extirpation.

*Extract of a secret letter from the Governor-Ge-
neral and Council of Bengal, dated Jan. 15,
1776.*

" We thought it adviseable to fix a proper
" weight and standard to be invariably ob-
" served by the Raja in all money which
" might be coined, on pain of FORFEIT-
" ING the Mint, and being liable to *any*
" PENALTY the Board might *think fit* to
" impose, on the *first* instance of any devia-
" tion."

Can the language of man convey in stron-
ger terms a clear explicit assumption of all
the rights and functions of Sovereign Power,
or a more full specification of the mode of
procedure to be applied to in cases of disobe-
dience, *Fine* and *Dispossession ?*—Rebellion,
surely, is a crime of as black a dye as adulte-
ration of coin ? But revolt was not a species
of guilt, which it was suspected that the Raja's
known dastardly nature and avaricious habits
would incline him, from any possible motives
of interest or policy, to commit. Debasing
of coin better suited with his genius and his
pursuits. Had he thus corrupted the channels
of commerce by a miserable fraud on the cre-
dulity

dulity of his people, he was to have been
fined for the benefit of his paramount: but
when the finews of Government are fhrunk
by his niggard obftinacy, when his deliberate
treafon endangers the very exiftence of our
Eaftern dominions, he is to be protefted
and excufed; his crime is to be palliated by
the voice of patriotifm at home; his punifhment to be mifconftrued into a flagrant aft of
violence. You and the public, I flatter myfelf, will fee the matter in a very different
light. Admitting that Cheyt Sing may be
morally vindicated for feizing the opportunity
of our embarrafiments to throw off his yoke,
Mr. Haftings is no lefs *morally* excufable for
difappointing his defign, and praife-worthy
for fo vigoroufly fupporting the interefts of
his conftituents. Cheyt Sing's expulfion from
his Zemindary had no relation to his intended fine, for he never knew the intention—
nor did he refift the fine, but the arreft. That
arreft furnifhed him with an unexpefted plea
for his pre-determined revolt, which, it is as
clear as the Sun, would have been promptly
executed, had the arreft never taken place.
He was infatuated—He had received bad
advice—I ftill think him to have been led

E 2   blindfold

blindfold to his own destruction. He had been taught to judge too lightly of the strength of our Government, and too favourably of his own. Independance was his object, and for that he forfeited his allegiance. But though he might have had a hoary Franklin at his elbow, he certainly had no Washington: the success which he never could hope from open hostilities, he sought by cowardly assassination. And when his attempt was defeated, when he could do no more mischief, and when the halter was already about his neck, he abjectly petitioned for the restoration of his wealth and territories in the despicable cant of slavish contrition. — The folly of his guilt can only be equalled by that of his repentance : had he been pardoned, his forgiveness would have been a pledge of impunity for the rebellion of every disaffected Zemindar in India. He was therefore expelled *of necessity;* or rather, his estates were *ipso facto* FORFEITED, from the instant that he took up arms : and it was but by an act of sovereign clemency, that the sequestered Zemindary was continued in his family.

The

The right of investiture having thus fully, efcheated to the Company, the terms by which Cheyt Sing had been bound were no longer obligatory on either party. The Zemindary is known to be fully adequate to a very large increase of rent, and the pressing exigencies of Government rendered an advance (in itself exceedingly moderate) an object of the utmost consequence. It was entirely fair and reasonable in the Governor-General to propose this addition to the revenue, and it was equally optional in the new Rajah to have refused investiture on those conditions; but as the demands of Government, even on the new leafe, bear no degree of comparison to the annual sum affessed on the lands, the present Zemindar has infinite cause to be pleased with his bargain.

Mr. Hastings might with great propriety, and in strict conformity to the feodal maxims of the Mogul Government, have demanded a large sum of money from the new Rajah, as a *Nuzzer*, or fine of renewal for his leafe. In proof of this, I appeal to the laft page but one of Appendix, No. 14, to the fixth report of the Select Committee of laft session, wherein

wherein is quoted an anfwer from the Roy-Royan, and Canongoes, (who are in the fame place explained to be *competent judges* of the cuftoms of the country, and of the ufages of the former Government) to certain queftions propounded to them in 1773, by the late Prefident and Council of Bengal, refpecting the inheritable tenure of Zemindaries. " It " is ufual for the fon of a Zemindar, after " his father's death, to repair to the prefence, " and *prefent a Nuzzer* to the King, *that a* " *new Sunnud may be made out* in his name."— A very little knowledge of Indian affairs will fuffice to underftand, that this *Nuzzer of renewal* is always proportionate to the fuppofed value of the lands, and does not, at the fame time, impede the ftipulation of an additional yearly rent: fo that the Governor-General has here, in a very diftinguifhed manner, exercifed the *reigning* virtue, *moderation*, by obtaining an eafy advance on the rent only, without proceeding to the *legal* and cuftomary extremity of a *fine of renewal.*— On the whole a traitor has been punifhed as he deferved; his ufelefs hoards have been brought into the mafs of general circulation ; his fucceffion is fo much clear gain to the

new

new Rajah, and the Company's affairs are
affifted in a critical moment by a fair and
equitable augmentation of revenue. All
parties are benefited at the expence of a
villain and a murtherer. His *caufe*, I truft,
will now experience the fate of his perfon.——

The grounds on which the attack on the
fecret article propofed to have been inferted
in a treaty with the Raja of Berar, will probably proceed, I have taken from the twenty-
third refolation of the Secret Committee,
read in the Houfe of Commons, on Monday,
April 15, 1782. On that queftion I believe
ftronger grounds of objeftion do not exift,
or the learned mover of the refolutions would
affuredly have brought them forward—thefe,
therefore, fuch as they now ftand, I fhall beg
leave with fubmiffion to canvafs.—In the firft
place, this *fecret article* of the treaty with
Boofla never came to a preliminary difcuffion.:
It lies buried in the fame grave with that
excellent young man whofe untimely death
prevented the negotiation. We now talk of
that article as if it had been of public noto-
riety, whereas it never was divulged in India ;
nor was it meant to be included in the treaty,

if

if Booſla could have been brought to any
terms of alliance without it. Moſt certain it
is, that the Nizam never entertained a ſuſpicion of its exiſtence, or traces of it would
be found in his expoſtulatory correſpondence
with the two Preſidencies: yet we are baited
with the hazardous " conſequence of an of-
" fenſive alliance with the Rajah of Berar,
" for the expreſs purpoſe of recovering for
" him the conqueſts made by the Nizam, and,
" of uniting the dangerous powers of the
" Mahratta empire under one active com-
" mand."—Theſe are arguments *ad captandum
vulgus*—the timorous forebodings of pruden-
tial politics. Mr. Haſtings is a ſtateſman on a
higher ſcale : and his genius, like that of Au-
guſtus over Antony's, looks down with an eye
of unerring penetration on the ſouls of the
Aſiatic Princes, and anticipates the ſtroke that
ſhall fruſtrate their deſigns. We may wrangle
and dogmatize here on the probable bias of
contingent events, and magnify the formidable reſult of the Nizam's reſentment, or
Booſla's ambition ; but the Governor-General
laughs at their pitiful manœuvres. The ſame
hand that plays the pawn, can throw the
king off the board with one ſlight touch of
the

the finger : its importance is only among bits of wood or ivory of its own form and order. I argue, firft, that the propofed treaty with the Raja of Berar was not for the *exprefs* pur- pofe of recovering for him what had been feized by the Nizam, but for the *exprefs pur- pofe* of fecuring to ourfelves a neceffary reve- nue and a fubftantial barrier on the weftern fide of India : Secondly, that at the time of propofing *that* treaty, the Nizam's fingle power was of little or no weight in the poli- tical fcale, and that his confequence confifts in the prudence with which he has contrived to appear prepared for war, without engaging in actual hoftilities. His *forte* lies in the Ca- binet, and the late confederacy of the Indian Powers is his mafter-piece. But had Boofla and his Mahratta friends been the avowed an- tagonifts of that league, inftead of its parties, the Nizam's wifdom muft have fought fome frefh fubterfuge for his own fafety. " The " union of the Mahratta Empire under one " active command," is juft as little to be dreaded. We have now for fome years fup- ported a war againft all the Mahratta States but Berar on the one hand, while Hyder Ally (formidable even to the combined forces of '

F   thofe

thofe very Mahrattas) has exerted all his
ftrength againft us on the other. Even fhould
we allow Boofla to have obtained his objeƐ
in confequence of our propofed treaty : füp-
pofe him to have weakened the Nizam, united
the Mahrattas, and fettled with us;—where
fhould we have been more vulnerable tĥan at
prefent ?—And who could have guaranteed to
Boofla, the loyal and unfhaken adherence of all
the reftlefs, ambitious, and intriguing Chiefs
of the Mahratta States to his ftandard ? The
fame policy which could detach Mhadajee
Scindia from the combination of his countrymen, and at one effort convert him from an
enemy to a moft ufeful ally, would foon con-
trive the means to diffever any other fimilar
confederacy. But the Governor-General,
knew that fuch an union would naturally fof-
ter in itfelf the feeds of its own diffolution.
The politics of Afia have in faƐ undergone
an entire revolution within a few centuries.
Of the four mighty Empires which once fhared
the whole between them, that of China alone
ftands undiminifhed. The thrones of the
Tartar, the Perfian, and the Mogul, are fallen, never to rife again. Their territories are
fubdivided, and the magic chain, which
bound

bound together and rivetted their authority, is vanifhed into air. For myfelf, I attribute this phenomenon entirely to the difcovery of the Cape of Good Hope, and to the improvement of navigation. Whether an imperceptible change of opinions and manners may have been formed by the gradual operation of commercial intercourfe, or by the influence of what other inftrument this levelling fyftem may have been promoted, I do not attempt to explain: but the *caufe* ftrikes me with the ftrongeft conviction, and I am more implicitly confirmed in my fentiments, when I confider the prefent condition of China.— Thofe commercial prohibitions, by which *one port only* is fuffered to admit foreign veffels through the whole aftonifhing extent of that empire, are to me the pledges of its duration. Should it once admit fhips and colonies indifcriminately,—*actum eft de Republica.*—I am therefore inclined to think, that Afia will never again fee another very powerful and extenfive monarchy of any continuance, under a feries of Afiatic Princes; and of all events, which can intereft my countrymen in India, the union of all the Mahrattas feems to me the leaft to be apprehended. After all, we need

fear

fear neither any single power, nor any combination of native powers in Afia; *while the sea is our own:* so long we shall predominate by land, and no longer. Naval strength is like the island of Laputa; it commands dominion by neceffity of fituation. While men muft either march or fail to conqueft, the latter will always beat; and if flying be among the arts yet difcoverable by man, that nation which fhall invent it, and preferve the fecret, will probably, for a time, rule over the habitable globe. —Had we laft year cavilled lefs about the interior arrangements of Indian affairs, and difpatched five fhips of the line more to that quarter in proper time, we might now have affumed a tone of irrefiftable fuperiority in our negociations with the French for a participation of Indian territories. If the Raja of Berar, by our affiftance, had weakened the Nizam, we fhould no longer have heard of the danger of incurring *his* vengeance; and if we had been clofely allied to thefe United Mahratta States, we had nothing to fear from *them*, till the alliance was broken. But even on that fuppofition, had the Mahratta powers attained to that formidable confiftency,

fiftency, fuggefted by the Penman of the Secret Committee's refolutions, the other native Princes of India, would moft eagerly have embraced a combination with us, to counteract the effects of their encroachments: fo that in the very effort of raifing the Mahrattas, we fhould have enfured to ourfelves the means of fecurity from their ingratitude. But the field of political conjecture is unlimited; its paths perplexing and uncertain. —It would be beft to leave the fairy land of hypothefis to that refpectable veteran, whofe peculiar province it is to give the graces of manly eloquence to the apologues of infantine fimplicity; who, after having ineffectually tried his verfatile weapon on the firft naval character the world ever faw, and on a commander, whofe laurels the very blaft of adverfity hath not been able to blight, now wields it with two-handed impetuofity againft the Chatham of the Eaft. But *here* alfo, he will not find the conflict more eafy, nor the victory more fecure than in his former attacks. To charges of criminality, the defence will be fhort, clear, and fatisfactory. We wait with confidence for the trial. If it be urged, that Mr. Haftings has involved

the

the Company in expenfive and unneceffary
wars, we appeal to the records at the India-
Houfe—to the reports and appendixes of two
Committees, and on their authority refute
the accufation. If it be faid, that he hath
loft the confidence of the country powers;
we anfwer, " that as far as prefumptive proof
" can be obtained, on fo complicated a mat-
" ter, we are warranted in afferting, that
" many of the firft Potentates of India, and
" in particular the Nabob Vizier of Oude,
" the Raja of Berar, the Nabob of the
Carnatic, and the Nizam have, in many
" and very ftreng inftances, manifefted
" their perfect reliance on his integrity and
" honour."—Finally, if it be fuggefted,
that he hath forfeited the national character
for moderation, we beg leave to premife
upon the argument, " that moderation is
" no part of our *national* character in
" Afia;" and we wi'l afterwards deny, that
the Governor-General hath in any degree
forfeited our claim to that virtue. While
we were known in India but as a Company
of Merchants, while we fubfifted by the
nicer barter of commodities, and fought by
affumed affability the preference of a mar-
ket, it cannot be fuppofed that our *national*
character

character was an object of confideration. It was our *commercial character* on which we relied for fuccefs, and our behaviour was naturally fuited to the fubordination of our circumftances. It was Clive who gave us our firft exiftence as a *nation* in the Eaft, and Clive's virtues were not of the pitiful negative clafs. Valour and conduct formed the bafis of his pile; juftice and honour were the cement of the fuperftructure. *Then* it was that we exchanged the pliability of mercantile negotiation for the fteadinefs of political independence; that we acquired the character of a brave, a fteady, and a generous people. If we are ftill to be confidered as mere merchants at home, it is but juft : here we poffefs neither kingdoms, nor revenues, nor armies: but we are not, on that account, to be deprived of our rights and privileges, warranted to us both by law and charter. If by that moderation which we are inftructed to practice, it be meant that we fhould again reduce ourfelves to our original ftate of traders in India, we reply, " That our *national cha-* " *racter* among Indians will not be at all " improved by a meer compromife of power " among ourfelves, and by fubftituting a

" Governor-

" Governor-General of Bengal on the part
" of the Crown, for him appointed by the
" Company."—But the language of Miniftry
is, that it is *expedient* to remove the prefent
Governor-General: and who fhall fix that
fhifting Proteus *expediency*, to bring him to
clofe examination?—It will be faid, that Mr.
Haftings's recall will procure an immediate ceffa-
tion of hoftilities in Afia.—The means however
feem very inadequate to the end propofed.
There are, as I think, but two methods of bring-
ing an obftinate enemy to terms: the one is by
victory—the other by conceffion. For the
former, no man can be more amply qualified than Sir Eyre Coote: he is the idol of
his army, the infpiring genius of the field, and
under him a Seapoy is fomewhat more
than an Afiatic. The latter method may be
deemed more confiftent with the prefent *mo-
derating principles*: but its *fafety* is yet very
far from demonftration. If conqueft be
within the powers of humanity, we need not
look farther for it than to Coote: but he
never could have taken the field, nor would
he have maintained his poft a fingle day without the wonderful affiftance and fupplies furnifhed him by the Governor-General of Bengal:

gal : and it will at leaft be a matter of much
difficulty to find a man more fertile in refources, and more gifted with the powers of
civil exertion, than Mr. Haftings; A new
Governor, we are told, would be more *moderate* in the articles on which he would agree
to a peace. But we have not yet inconteftably
afcertained the *ultimatum* of Mr. Haftings's
political *moderation.* His fucceffor would
probably be a ftranger to the internal ftrength,
to the relative advantages and private views of
the different States of India ; in their language
he muft be totally deficient : and at all events,
will be reduced to the neceffity of acting upon
the dictates of fubfidiary knowledge. He will
fee all things through a cloud, and at fecond
hand. The prefent Governor-General can
hear, and fpeak, and judge for himfelf. While
we condemn his want of moderation, we for-
get that this very conduct may be founded on
the meer principles of public prefervation.—
It is probable enough, that he may have fo
accurately compared our exigencies with our
means, as to have feen the abfolute impoffibility as well as impropriety of conceffion.—
We have a large eftablifhment, an increafing
demand for money, and a heavy debt ;
it furely would not be prudent *(even in a na-*
G   *tional*

tional view, as long as the old adage " *salus populi suprema lex esto*," shall be found policy) to admit of such a peace as should leave us no human chance of ever reducing our incumbrances! A peace founded on the voluntary dereliction of those exprefs objects for which we have so long contended, would prove no lefs faithlefs than difreputable. An acknowledgment of pr efent inferiority would but provoke future demands; and if we concede any thing now for the fake of tranquillity, the moment our enemies shall have recruited their strength, they will again commence hoftilities, in hopes of farther conceffions. To clofe the war, without fettling the balance of power, would but expofe the fcale to the perpetual chance of new vibrations from the flightest accident: we have nearly obtained poffeffion of the beam, and why should we wantonly reject it? The prefent ftruggles may be compofed on a fyftem that shall preferve the calm of all our Afiatic connexions for half a century, or they may be fufpended by an infidious truce, which all the parties will be forward to break. I will hazard a conjecture, which I dare flatter myfelf, Sir, You will not wholly reject. Negotiations for a general peace in Europe have been

for

for fome time on the tapis: among the various reafons imagined for their pro-traction, a difference with regard to the parti-cipation of territories in India is the moft generally received. The French are thought to fpin out the preliminaries, in hopes that fome unfavourable turn of our affairs in the Carnatic may enable them to dictate more humiliating terms. Now I have not a doubt, but if our legiflature, at the firft opening of the prefent feffion, had fuddenly recalled Mr. Haftings, and infifted on his quitting the chair on the inftant arrival of his fucceffor, that the Cabinet of Verfailles would abruptly have broken off the treaty, and have trufted more to the effects of our ill-timed refolution, than to their own arms, *(an object which I think them to have ftill in view)* for the event of another Indian campaign. Our new Governor, Sir, were he to defcend from heaven in their fight, would excite diftruft in fome of our allies, fear in many, and an expectation of change in all. Intereft would induce fome to ftipulate for frefh advantages as the price of their alliance: apprehenfion would perfuade others to ftand neuter, until they fhould have feen the pro-bable confequences of the new Governor's

conduct

conduct. A circumstance which thus damped the ardour of our friends, would in the same degree add vigour to the exertions of our adversaries. Chance at least would be in their favour. They have beholden but Clive and Haftings, on whose side destiny itself seemed to contend, and they know as well as ourselves that extraordinary men do not use to spring up like mushrooms. On the whole, this doctrine of *expediency*, which is now to be the engine for Mr. Haftings's removal, was the very plea for his continuation, at the last General Court of Proprietors. I appeal to the protefts of the diffentient Directors, I appeal to the nervous and irrefiftable eloquence of the day's debate, whether any reason be so forcibly urged, or so decidedly conclusive, as that of the neceffity for prolonging the authority of the present Governor-General, *on account of the very perplexed ftate of our affairs.* This is the argument on which he has been supported by his immediate employers, it is now the charge on which he is to be degraded. Admirable pliability of language, which (as we are told of a Hebrew word that may fignify either to blefs or to curfe) can fave at one end of the town and damn at the other! Like the ob-
literated

literated characters of fome illegible infcrip-
'tion, that fuit 'equally with an Otho or an
old button, a Roman fhield, or a rufty
pot-lid! -

When Mr. Haftings's recall fhall have been
irrevocably doomed by the whole legiflative
power, the bufinefs of *expediency* is ftill but
half accomplifhed. The greater moiety of
the tafk is to find another Governor-General
more fit for our purpofe, and to eftablifh him
in our opinions on the bafis of conviction.
If You be diffatisfied with the capacity of
your bailiff or fteward, you difmifs him, I
grant, but not till you have feen another
whofe character you approve on a clofe en-
quiry, and whofe abilities you afcertain to be
fuch as will fuit you, by the manner in which
he has been ufed to exercife them. A Governor-General is the fteward of the Company: his capacity muft be fuited to the
nature of his office, and be broken in to its
functions by experience. The bungling work
made by General Clavering and his majority,
the glaring abfurdities obtruded on the public
by Mr. F——, after fix years refidence in
the habits of bufinefs, have given the Company a furfeit of *experimental government*;
and

" Circuit, and the countenance given by him
" to very improper meafures, on . feveral
" occafions, relative to the letting of the
" diftricts, deferve the ftrongeft marks of our
" difpleafure ; *but as thofe fubjects were foreign*
" *to the General s military profeffion,* we fhall
" not, on the prefent occafion, proceed fur-
" ther, than to exprefs our difapprobation
" of his conduct."—Another inftance I find
in Appendix, No. 3, to the firft report of
the Select Committee of laft feffion.
Extract from General Sir Eyre Coote's
minute, in confultation, 24th Oct. 1780.

" As the determining upon points, relative
" to law proceedings, has fallen fo little
" *within the limits of my profeffion,* I acknow-
" ledge myfelf *inadequate* to the forming a
" thorough judgment, concerning the plan
" propofed by the Governor - General."—
Here then, we have one of the Company's
Commanders in Chief acquitted of refponfi-
bility for errors of the firft importance in
revenue matters, on account of his *profeffion.*
Another, whofe fervices have but this inftant
been honoured with the thanks of both
Houfes, and *who was once* (as I have heard)
a Candidate for the Government of Bengal,
pleads *his profeffion* in apology for not enter-
ing into the difcuffion of a legal arrangement.

Yet

Yet revenue, at least, is the first concern of the Bengal administration, and frequent occasions will arise for the exercise of a tried judgment, on questions of coinage, of commerce, of civil and political negociation, of practical government, and of legiflation. Far be it from me to suggest, and I do from my soul renounce the idea, that any one of those noble and honourable perfons, whom the conjectures of the public have, at different times, named for the fucceffion to that high office, be not amply qualified for the task. While I allow them every advantage of natural and acquired abilities, I am within the pale of refpect, when I venture to hint, that experience may be wanting to the completion of their characters : nor do I think that any one of them could more effectually confult his own honour, as well as his duty to his country, than by dedicating a portion of his time, to the habits of feeing with his own eyes, and of judging upon his own knowledge, before he launches out to act upon his own bottom.

I have now, Sir, only to beg pardon for the length of this intrufion : its defign, I am fure, You will not condemn. If it fhould

H   in

in the fmalleft degree ferve the Company, whofe interefts I have moft warmly at heart, and a man for whofe merit I have the moft profound veneration, I fhall very heartily rejoice: fhould it by any means ferve my country, even at the expence of thofe objects which induced me to take up the pen, I fhall ftill have a confcious pride in my labour: fhould it fail in all points to be ferviceable, and fhare the common oblivion of diurnal publications, i have yet the flattering affurance of your promifed exertions in the fame caufe, to give new life to my expectations, and to dart a fplendor where I have but raifed a mift.

I have the honour to remain,

S I R,

Your moft obedient fervant,

DETECTOR.

4th of January, 1783.

www.ingramcontent.com/pod-product-compliance
Lightning Source LLC
Chambersburg PA
CBHW031810090426
42739CB00008B/1236